Leadership

Develop The Necessary Leadership Qualities And
Interpersonal Abilities For Management Success

(The World's Most Successful Entrepreneurs: Lessons)

Jean-Francois

TABLE OF CONTENT

Chapter 1: A Female-Specific Leadership Style 1

Chapter 2: Work Skills 7

Chapter 3: What Does A Leader Entail? 10

Chapter 4: How To Sustain A High Performance Culture: Developing A Leadership Attitude 16

Chapter 5: Constructing A Solid Group 27

Chapter 6: Thinking Ability 47

Chapter 7: A Discussion Of Leadership 56

Chapter 9: Achievement Of Objectives: The Power Of Motivation And Dedication 66

Chapter 10: Leadership Is Internal 77

Chapter 11: On The Shoulders Of Titans 82

Chapter 12: How Do You Attract Precisely What You Desire? 87

Chapter 13: The Importance Of Leadership Principles 95

Chapter 14: What Is Business Culture? 100

Chapter 15: Other Assessment Systems 105

Chapter 16: Goal Setting 108

Chapter 17: You Must Understand That Your Goal Is Greater Than Your Challenges.. 113

Chapter 1: A Female-Specific Leadership Style

The importance of feminine leadership styles in contemporary society is heightened by their emphasis on collaboration, compassion, equality, and growth. In terms of emotional intelligence and competitive soft skills, such as mentoring, conflict resolution, critical thinking, and organizational awareness, women excel. Managing and leading a successful business requires technical expertise, but empowering your workforce is equally important. In addition to outperforming men in terms of emotional intelligence, women also outnumber men in enrollment and graduation from college or university, and they are more likely to pursue a postgraduate degree to advance their professional abilities (Sharma, 2020). Another "hidden" or unrecognized talent possessed by many female leaders is the ability to employ household management skills to the workplace.

It goes without saying that not all women have children or manage households, but a large number of them do, and often, a disproportionate amount of household work and child care has fallen on the shoulders of mothers. Mothers have always labored, but their unpaid domestic labor and child-rearing duties have been undervalued for decades. Even today, household labor is rarely accorded the same respect and recognition as formal labor; however, the skills acquired while managing a household and providing for children can assist mothers in their professional contexts (and are particularly advantageous in "family-like" organizations). In order to manage a household, a business, or a group of employees, one must have the ability to rapidly adapt to changing environments, delegate tasks based on time, skill, and adaptability, manage a variety of tasks, and be patient when assisting others. As a mother (of four children!), I am familiar with the challenges of operating a business while juggling housework, childcare, meal preparation, and everything else involved in raising a family. It's challenging, but achievable!

As a result of the demands of their labor, many mothers experience exhaustion or even fatigue. In truth, 42% of women in heterosexual, dual-career relationships experience burnout, while 46% of women in such relationships with young children report similar feelings (Chen et al., 2021). In addition to being assessed for requesting flexible work arrangements, these mothers report feeling judged. As women leaders who want their business to thrive and also want to empower their employees, it is of the uttermost importance to consider the unique struggles of women employees (especially those with children).

Establishing and maintaining a sustainable work-life balance for yourself (as a leader) and your employees can be accomplished in three straightforward ways: implementing flexible work schedules and norms, providing and encouraging the use of benefits, and serving as a mentor or positive role model for others. For instance, flexible working hours may include the option to work from home, the hosting of meetings and events on virtual platforms, and the encouragement of employees to design their own schedules. This permits employees, particularly those with children, to schedule their work around their child care obligations (such as school drop-off and pick-up times). In addition, a successful and inspiring leader must encourage employees to take frequent, brief breaks to prevent burnout. The distinctively female or feminine style of leadership affords female CEOs, managers, and entrepreneurs the opportunity to alter the status quo and lead businesses and corporations into "the new normal." A new norm that prioritizes employee well-being and professional (and personal) development, establishes new and more flexible working norms, and accepts and embraces work-life balance.

How then do women exert their leadership authority and self-assurance without compromising their femininity? We can begin by questioning our own gender biases. You did indeed read that accurately. As women, our own gender bias has been handed down for generations, and this deeply ingrained, often subconscious programming means that we, too, can impose gender stereotypes and norms on ourselves and others. We may judge our female supervisor unfairly for being too soft-spoken or too loud, too aggressive or too submissive. Even so, we may self-regulate our behavior, facial expressions, and tone of voice so as not to appear aggressive, authoritative, or emotive. This nearly daily routine is taxing! Then, we will be able to challenge our own negative self-talk and the burden we place on ourselves to conform to unhealthy gender norms. In addition, if we devote so much time to evaluating other female leaders, we will have no opportunity to collaborate with them.

Reminding yourself that femininity is not synonymous with inferiority is an integral part of adopting a feminine leadership style and boosting your self-confidence. It does not even have to prevent you from achieving your professional objectives. Feminine leadership styles are gaining popularity in organizations, particularly those that value cooperation and collaboration over individualism, so we must continually emphasize the advantages of such leadership in today's society. By doing so, we will be able to increase our self-confidence and motivate others to be the best versions of themselves.

Chapter 2: Work Skills

It is encouraging to learn that an adolescent is succeeding in school and has a promising future ahead. Teens who perform well in school can obtain numerous opportunities and benefits, such as admission to a prestigious college or university, a high-paying employment, and the ability to pursue their passions. Work skill acquisition is a distinct ballgame. Teens should begin preparing for life after school because obtaining their dream employment may be difficult. As early as feasible, preteens should learn how to fill out a job application, prepare for an interview, and respond to interview questions.

There are norms to which you must become accustomed in the workplace.

Arrive on time: It is essential to arrive on time for your task and meetings at work. This demonstrates reverence for your employer and coworkers and ensures that you are able to fulfill your duties and obligations.

Dress appropriately: In the majority of workplaces, dress codes dictate what constitutes appropriate attire. It is essential for a teen to comprehend and adhere to these principles, as failure to do so may be perceived as disrespectful or unprofessional.

Respect and courtesy are essential in the workplace. Respect and courtesy must be shown to your employer, coworkers, and patrons. This includes the use of polite language, courtesy, and attentiveness.

In the workplace, it is essential to obey the instructions and directives of your supervisor or manager. This includes carrying out tasks as instructed and adhering to safety regulations and procedures.

In the majority of occupations, it is essential to work well with others and make a positive contribution to the team. This may include assisting your coworkers, offering assistance when required, and collaborating on projects. Flexibility and adaptability are essential in the workplace. This may involve working different hours or taking on new responsibilities as required.

It is often advantageous in the workplace to take initiative and be proactive in your work. This may involve proposing new ideas, assuming additional responsibilities, or offering assistance in areas where you observe a need.

To be successful in the workplace, a teenager will need to know and exercise a variety of crucial skills and behaviors. Teenagers must be willing to learn and acclimate to the rules and expectations of the workplace and be prepared to do so. While still in high school, teens can prepare for the responsibilities of a prospective career through summer or part-time employment. Teachers can introduce these concepts to adolescents, as well as compose a list of places where they can gain work experience.

Chapter 3: What Does A Leader Entail?

The term "leader" can evoke various mental images. For example:

A political leader pursuing a profoundly personal cause. An explorer venturing into the wilderness. An executive developing strategies to achieve organizational objectives.

Different perspectives exist regarding who can and should lead. Instead of the traditional "top-down" approach, management professor Michael Useem argued that leadership is most effective when it originates from the bottom up. Moreover, leadership can originate from a variety of sources in today's complex, globalized workplaces. In fact, the supervisory leaders may be able to have the most influence in certain enterprises. Managers are the ones who collaborate most closely with teams.

No longer is leadership viewed as a solitary endeavor. Given that many businesses today are too large and complex for a single leader to manage alone, the paradigm of distributed leadership, which has its origins in education, is gaining popularity.

Module 2: Determining Your Leadership Style: Evaluating and Enhancing Your Skills

Each individual has a unique leadership style, and there is no single best method to lead. In reality, the majority of people are a combination of multiple leadership styles, depending on the situation or the individual they are leading. Nevertheless, it can be useful to determine which of these styles feels most natural to you so that you can learn how to better your skills in areas where you feel weak or where you need to develop. By determining your personal leadership style, you can establish clear objectives and standards for self-improvement, as well as determine the type of environment that will be most conducive to your style.

The Five Elements

To determine your leadership style, you must do more than answer a few yes-or-no queries. It entails examining numerous facets of your life, evaluating your behavior in each circumstance, and determining which aspects are most important to you. Once you are aware of this, it is simpler to evaluate potential work situations through the same lenses and determine whether they align with your priorities.

Visionary and idealistic - This trait entails seeing opportunities where others do not. You're able to envision a desirable future state for an organization or initiative, and then persuade others to join you. People with high visionary/idealistic scores are typically visionary, optimistic, and energizing leaders who can inspire those around them. They also tend to be excellent at generating new ideas, but struggle with implementation and execution due to a lack of follow-through skills.

2. Affiliative: As an affiliative leader, you are primarily concerned with fostering relationships and preserving harmony within your team or organization as a whole. You excel at encouraging collaboration and working with others to achieve shared objectives. People with a high affiliation score tend to be empathetic leaders who are skilled at resolving conflicts and ensuring that their teams function well together. They have a tendency to be extremely people-oriented, which can sometimes hinder their decision-making because they care more about being liked than respected.

This component concentrates on creating opportunities for others to contribute ideas, opinions, and suggestions, and then implementing those ideas that you believe will benefit all parties involved in a project or business endeavor. People who score highly in democratic leadership tend to be excellent at empowering their teams and fostering teamwork. They are frequently highly creative leaders who can generate new ideas and implement them once they have been decided. As a result of requiring input from all parties involved prior to moving forward with plans, they may occasionally struggle to make decisions.

4. Commanding/authoritative - As a commanding leader, you are primarily concerned with getting things done effectively and efficiently, which frequently necessitates making snap decisions without regard for what others may think. High scorers on commanding leadership are typically decisive leaders with strong problem-solving skills and the ability to make difficult decisions when necessary. They are excellent at coming up with inventive solutions to problems, but they can sometimes appear intimidating or overbearing

because they do not seek the opinions of others prior to making decisions.

5. Pacesetting/controlling - This component concentrates on motivating your team by establishing ambitious objectives that push everyone out of their comfort zones and toward excellence. High scorers on pacesetting leadership tend to be highly motivated leaders who appreciate pushing themselves and their teams to achieve more than they believed possible prior to beginning a new project or business venture.

Chapter 4: How To Sustain A High Performance Culture: Developing A Leadership Attitude

Some individuals hold the view that leaders are born, not made. Certainly, it is conceivable that some of us possess characteristics that make us good leaders. However, leadership can be acquired regardless of one's nature. Beyond words and deeds, leadership is about having a particular perspective on situations. Therefore, everyone is capable of developing a leadership mindset. Additionally, when we exercise our leadership abilities, they become a habit. In this chapter, we will attempt to comprehend how individual contributors and administrators can traverse the path to leadership.

MANAGEMENT VERSUS LEADERSHIP

Individual contributors are primarily concerned with their performance, collaboration with other team members, and positive relationships with their managers. Being a manager entails a unique set of responsibilities. Historically, there were distinctions between executives and managers, but these distinctions are now blurring.

Management consists primarily of directing team members in their duties. When employees feel confused, unmotivated, or misdirected, they turn to their supervisors, who instruct them on what to do and how to do it. In other words, it involves ensuring that things are completed correctly. You are responsible for the planning, organization, and direction of tasks as a manager. You must also monitor the performance of your team members and assist them if they encounter difficulties along the path.

Leadership goes above and beyond. First, a leader is accountable for the team's or organization's overarching strategy and vision. Your vision for the team can make or break their prospects for success. A leader must also comprehend what genuinely motivates their followers. What are their hopes and desires? What brings them joy? What are their greatest obstacles? These questions, when answered truthfully, will help you determine whether the vision of your team aligns with your own. It will also make it simpler for you to assign roles and responsibilities to team members in a manner that maximizes their likelihood of success. Consequently, a leader does not merely supervise the execution of ideas, but also ensures that the ideas are worthwhile to begin with.

Recognizing the Major Distinctions Between Leadership and Management

Here, we will examine the distinctions between traditional management and leadership approaches.

Typically, managers are expected to be problem-solvers. They are expected to be task-focused, demonstrating to their teams how to achieve daily peak performance. They are also expected to be rational and determined. They must analyze the problems their teams are facing and provide solutions. On the other hand, leaders are frequently described as having large personalities and tremendous charisma. They are required to inspire their employees with optimism for the future. Since leaders set the vision for their teams, their greatest strengths are their creativity and willingness to take calculated risks. A manager is typically task-oriented, whereas a leader is typically people-oriented. It's a win-win situation for both team members and administrators when tasks are accomplished efficiently. However, the function of a leader extends far beyond task completion.

"A leader is someone who knows the path, walks the path, and demonstrates the path" (John C. Maxwell, n.d.). Therefore, to be an effective leader, you must have a vision and communicate it to your team, set a good example, and support your team as they pursue their individual and collective success.

Due to their responsibility for execution, managers are the ones who establish schedules and empower their teams to excel at their assigned tasks. A manager is also typically perceived to be risk-averse. What does this signifier? Since a manager must provide analytical solutions to problems, they are concerned with minimizing risks and maximizing success. On the other hand, a leader is expected to take risks. Because with great hazards come great rewards. In addition to being analytical in their approach, they are expected to be creative problem-solvers. It is expected that they will use their ability to think laterally to generate creative solutions. In other words, they must challenge the limits of their team's capabilities.

You are expected to be more involved in the daily activities and concerns of your team as a manager. A leader is expected to be more facilitative, which requires them to encourage their team members to determine how best to achieve their objectives on their own. A transactional relationship can exist between a manager and their team members. In other words, a manager's work is accomplished so long as the task is completed. This does not imply that a manager cannot have deeper relationships with their subordinates; it simply means that a manager can exist without subordinates. A leader must develop close bonds with their team members. They can have a transformative effect on their organizations, but only if they appeal to something profound within themselves.

Management is technically a position of authority, whereas leadership is a position of influence. As a manager, you may discover that people defer to you due to your position of authority. Even if you are not in a conventionally superior position to them, people will look to you for guidance and inspiration if you are a leader. Managers appeal to the intellect by requesting that their teams adhere to logic and reason. Leaders appeal to the emotions, igniting fervor in their teams. It is obvious which has the greater impact.

The Importance of Managers Becoming Leaders

I have previously stated that the distinctions between management and leadership are blurring. This implies that employees have higher expectations of their managers. What is the cause of this change? We reflect on how the nature of labor has evolved.

Historically, workers viewed their employment primarily as a source of security and convenience. As long as they received their salary at the end of the week or month and the working conditions were acceptable, they did not have many other expectations. This is also due to the fact that there was greater job security in the past. The majority of individuals remained with the same organization their entire careers. Therefore, they need to know their job profile, whether they performed well throughout the year, and whether there were any areas in which they needed to develop. Therefore, they desired a competent supervisor and were satisfied with annual performance assessments.

Now, the majority of workers strongly identify with their employment. They are not satisfied with performing their designated tasks and receiving compensation. They desire workplaces that are superior and more inclusive. They desire leaders who are accountable to them. They want to know whether the vision of their company aligns with their own. Greater emphasis is placed on their passion and purpose. This indicates that they care more about their careers than their employment. What are the implications for managers?

Managers must establish rapport with their subordinates. They should have more frequent and in-depth conversations about their professions, aspirations, and dreams. They must now act as coaches for their team members, discussing methods to aid in their professional and personal development. In addition, there is a greater emphasis on discussions regarding work-life balance, which requires managers to view their team members in a more holistic manner. Clearly, managers can no longer achieve success without leadership skills.

Consider whether You are a Leader or a Manager.

Despite the fact that leadership cannot always be reduced to a checklist, there are certain questions you can ask yourself to determine if you are a leader.

If you did not occupy a formal position of authority, would your team members listen to you? Do you believe you can influence people's opinions on a subject through your knowledge and communication skills? Do individuals gravitate towards you for advice? Do you stand out as someone who can effectively solve problems and motivate others? One way to answer these questions is to determine whether you are frequently approached by individuals from outside your orbit of authority. Do they still view you as a leader when someone's salary or career advancement is no longer dependent on you?

Typically, do you participate in ensuring that people complete their designated tasks effectively, or do you exceed your mandate? Do you discuss the objectives of your employees with them? Are you familiar with the obstacles they face? Do you have an accurate understanding of their values and principles? Do you assist your employees in overcoming their shortcomings and capitalizing on their strengths? Together, our strengths and vulnerabilities determine whether or not we can complete a task successfully. Nevertheless, if we want to stand out and accomplish our mission, our strengths will get us there. When we conquer our weaknesses, we acquire the self-assurance necessary to perform at our best every day. Likewise, when we recognize our strengths, we obtain a competitive advantage over others. A genuine leader assists their followers on both fronts.

Do you find yourself focusing excessively on minor details? Do not misunderstand; I am not referring to having an eye for detail. Do you typically invest a great deal of time micromanaging your employees? Are you constantly holding your people's hands as opposed to occasionally taking a step back? Do you find it difficult to trust and delegate responsibilities to your employees? If you can appreciate the particulars without losing site of the big picture, you have leadership potential.

Chapter 5: Constructing A Solid Group

Assume that, as a manager, you have been asked to assemble a team for the completion of a specific project. How can you begin selecting relatives and organizing them into a cohesive group?

Carefully select the ideal individuals. Choose them based on their skills and capacities as they pertain to your specific project. You are not absolutely certain to require the individual top, but you do require it for your specific project. Concentrate on the skills you need most for the task at hand. Avoid being enticed by capabilities that you will never need.

You most likely require a variety of coworkers, each with a unique set of skills and capacities, as opposed to a succession of clones with identical abilities. Ensure that, collectively, they address all the skills you require to the extent you require them.

Try not to overlook the need to select individuals who can coexist and cooperate with one another. A gathering of divas is absolutely unnecessary. Additionally, you would need to establish the Vibe and Standard procedures.

A strong team is essential for the success of any endeavor or project because it fosters a positive and supportive culture and ensures that everyone is working towards the same objectives.

We will begin by discussing the significance of team formation and the role team dynamics play in the success of a project. We will also examine strategies for fostering collaboration and open communication, as well as for cultivating a positive team culture.

Power is the capacity to exert influence over other individuals and events. It is acquired by leaders as a result of their personalities, positions, and circumstances. For instance, the manager's authority over subordinates is derived from a variety of power bases, some of which are discussed below:

a) Coercive power - This type of power is based on fear and punishment threats. It is frequently used by executives to accomplish tasks. In an organization, employees labor tirelessly to avoid missing out on bonuses. This is done to avoid being questioned or fired. Some of them complete their tasks to avoid being yelled at by the manager. Presenters and producers in electronic media conform to the coercive authority of their superiors.

b) Legitimate power: This is positional power acquired through the formal authority granted to an individual by the top management or a superior authority in the hierarchy. The manager or principal assigns tasks to subordinates with instructions on how they are to be completed and expects his orders to be followed within the specified time frame. He has the legal authority to do so.

c) Referent power: This derives from the charismatic personal qualities of the leader. These qualities are limited by their subordinates due to the reverence they inspire. Staff members frequently admire certain managers for their enterprising nature, firmness, punctuality, and excellent dressing habits, etc., and consciously or subconsciously emulate them. Because he is admired and liked, this form of power enables the manager to obtain simple compliance with his wishes.

d) Expert Power: This refers to the power derived from the leader's pertinent expertise, skill, and job-related knowledge. Producers, presenters, and reporters respect and obediently follow leaders with extensive job knowledge. In addition, a person in the editorial department of a newspaper or the programming section of a television station may be influential due to his knowledge, even if he lacks the seniority to exercise formal authority.

e) recompense Power: This power grants an individual the authority to recompense subordinates who comply with his orders with promotions, recognition, and pay raises. This power basis is frequently the result of sycophancy and phony allegiance to staff and managers.

f) Connection Power: This is power derived from informal connections with eminent individuals who control a company's controlling shares. The manager's power base can be bolstered by his proximity to the owner, a prominent member of the board of directors, or even the managing director. Excessive use of connection power induces anxiety and, consequently, false loyalty, which can be counterproductive.

g) Political Power: This type of power derives from the support of group members. Some leaders in trade unions and politics, for instance, are elected to positions of authority. Because he is the chairman of the Journalists' Union, a reporter or programme production staff member may be feared or recognized by management. The position allows him to rally workers in support of or opposition to management policies, depending on the circumstances.

h) Information Power: The leader's liaison function between upper management and subordinates enables him to gather information about management plans and perspectives on particular issues. Therefore, he may manipulate subordinate by strategically releasing or withholding information. For instance, the manager and others may play politics with information in their possession to delay or expedite subordinate decision-making on particular matters.

How to Develop Your Leadership Capabilities

No matter your present skill level, there is always room for improvement. There are numerous strategies to enhance your leadership abilities. Practice is the most effective method to advance your skills to the next level.

There are opportunities to acquire experience every day, even outside of the workplace. Plan a family excursion for the weekend. Conduct a family gathering. Host and organize a celebration.

Utilize every leadership opportunity to enhance your abilities:

Create a vision and communicate it to your employees. Take the time necessary to determine the objective and the path to achieving it. The most effective goals have a deadline and a distinct indication of achievement.

‣ Outline the steps you will take to achieve the objective. Include everyone in the meeting of strategy. Consider the comments you receive.

‣ Demonstrate to team members how they will benefit from achieving the objective.

Demonstrate your values. Numerous team members are uncertain of what to anticipate from an unknown commander. Each individual has his or her own code of conduct. Let everyone know your position. Every choice you make is an illustration of your moral code.

‣ Your actions establish the standards for everyone else. Be confident enough to communicate your expectations to others.

Have a positive attitude. Even if the situation has deteriorated, keep your head up. Rarely will your team have a more positive demeanor than you do. Not only will you feel better, but your team will also perform better and feel more optimistic about the future.

Develop your communication abilities. These abilities are essential. Make every effort to improve your communication skills. Ask yourself the following questions frequently:

Does everyone understand what I expect of them?

Does everyone have the required information?

Can every member of the team accurately communicate the project's objective?

Am I attentive to the contributions of each team member?

Determine the most effective method to motivate each team member. This may require time to determine. At the very least, take the time to regularly encourage and compliment each team member.

Demonstrate your dedication to achieving success. You determine the commitment of your team members based on your own level of commitment.

- No one will be more concerned than you. You will labor harder than anyone else. Show how significant the endeavor is to you.
- Your dedication inspires others to work hard.

Be approachable, but serious. If you are endearing, others will strive to assist you. Are you not more likely to assist a friend than an adversary?

- Being affable is not synonymous with weakness. Maintain accountability, but be equitable. If you want others to take the endeavor seriously, you must take the project seriously yourself.

Maximize your strengths while delegating your weaknesses to your team. Rarely does a single individual possess all the necessary skills and abilities to complete a significant undertaking on their own. Stick to your strengths and allow those with the necessary abilities to fill in the gaps.

‣ Being at your finest inspires confidence in those around you. Admitting your weaknesses demonstrates your intelligence, humility, and dedication to success.

Develop and improve your abilities. The best method to improve your leadership abilities is to find a mentor whose skills you admire. There are alternative options if you cannot locate a suitable mentor.

‣ Books. Numerous volumes have been written on the topic of leadership. Examine those with the highest ratings and put them to use. Do not restrict yourself to a quick perusal. It is not only about acquiring knowledge. You must consistently implement the information to see improvement.

‣ Websites. Leadership is a prominent topic of discussion. There are enough complimentary articles and videos to keep you occupied forever.

Formalized instruction. The topic of leadership is covered in seminars, webinars, and even college courses.

‣ Anyone committed to becoming a more effective leader can discover the information necessary to advance their skills.

Practice leads to mastery. Utilize every opportunity to acquire and apply leadership skills. It is impossible to become an adept in anything without deliberate and sustained effort. Learn a little each day and implement it with vigor. Evaluate your outcomes and strive for improvement.

Few individuals make concerted efforts to develop their leadership abilities. You can rapidly surpass your peers if you put forth the necessary effort.

How to determine the kind of leader you are

At some point in our careers, we will all have to contend with leadership responsibilities. Whether we are in command of a small project or an entire department, we will eventually be responsible for rallying a group of people to solve a problem.

Despite the fact that there are right and wrong methods to lead, there is no one style that works for everyone. There are numerous ways to lead a group, and you should discover the style that best suits you and the objectives you wish to accomplish.

If you're an entrepreneur seeking to develop your leadership skills, here are six ways to determine your leadership style:

Recognize Your Individuality Traits

Assessing your personality is the only method to accurately determine the type of leader you are. Examine the dominant traits of your personality and observe how they manifest in a professional, social, or familial setting.

Consider the characteristics that your coworkers and acquaintances most frequently attribute to you. It is essential to evaluate your character in these situations in order to determine how you will lead a team. This is because our behavioral characteristics always influence our decision-making, interactions with others, and stress management.

Consider the factors that typically influence your decisions. Consider how frequently factors such as determination, impulsiveness, and patience influence your actions and decision-making. These queries will help you gain a deeper understanding of your thought process and leadership habits.

Consider Your Values

Values are behavior's measuring tools. These characteristics are the foundations of reputations. People use values to evaluate personalities, comprehend how another person thinks, and assess how they are perceived and treated.

Values help us determine whom we can rely on, how a person might respond to a given circumstance, and whom we want to carry our future. When employees are unable to identify their leader's fundamental values, they are not only more likely to doubt his or her abilities, but also to mistrust the leader's direction and agenda.

Respect, influence, authenticity, courage, and integrity are examples of fundamental values that influence your conscious and unconscious team leadership. Consider the values that inform your typical behavior. By focusing on your beliefs and values, you can enhance your understanding of your leadership qualities and skills.

Recognize Your Weaknesses

Strength-based leadership is not always as effective as one might believe. To be a genuinely great leader, you must comprehend your weaknesses and learn how they will impact your leadership position. Once identified, you can use this information to enhance your leadership approach.

This will not only assist you in addressing your deficiencies, but it will also help your team recognize your competence and authenticity. Transparency regarding the flaws you intend to surmount can motivate your team to improve themselves.

Ask for Feedback

You can take as many leadership personality tests as you like, but without feedback from those you lead, you will never acquire a complete understanding of the type of leader you are. Obtaining the opinions of your coworkers regarding your leadership style will provide you with valuable insight into behaviors you may have missed otherwise.

You will gain a deeper understanding of your personality traits, strengths, limitations, and perceived values by soliciting feedback from your team regarding your leadership abilities.

In addition, fostering a culture of feedback among your colleagues can help you enhance your team's communication and interactions. The most effective method to steer your company is by understanding how to better meet the needs of those around you.

Evaluate Your Capacity to Delegate

Sometimes it is difficult to let go. This is particularly true for leaders who have nurtured a company from its inception. Despite this, the ability to entrust others with intricate details is a strong indicator of leadership.

Consider the tasks you could delegate as you determine the type of leader you are and formulate a plan to enhance your leadership style. Social media management, web design, search engine optimization, and public relations are tasks that may be better adapted for other members of your team. Not only will delegating these tasks allow you to concentrate your efforts, but it will also help you build trust within your team.

Follow Your Leaders

The majority of individuals' characteristics are formed by those who wield influence over them. In the beginning, these individuals are our parents and teachers; ultimately, they become our bosses and managers. Whether we are aware of it or not, the characteristics of these influencers affect our decision-making, behavior under duress, and problem-solving.

As you attempt to determine what type of leader you are, consider the leaders in your life whose qualities are most similar to yours. While analyzing the skill sets of the leaders you have worked with, identify which of their characteristics have influenced your leadership role.

Understanding the ways in which you presently influence the company's culture will be facilitated by gaining insight into how you have applied these leadership qualities to your approach.

Chapter 6: Thinking Ability

Indeed, even the most difficult business decisions are colored by our own perspectives, and we evaluate the value of risks and benefits based on our human emotions, such as fear and confidence. Our decisions reflect our fundamental qualities and standards, thereby revealing who we truly are. They have strategies and devices in place to ensure that they have the greatest opportunity to exercise sound judgment.

The most serious problems in leadership occur when individuals allow their own emotions to dominate and disregard current realities: Either the situation is not accurately analyzed, and fundamental realities are missing, or the leader disregards current realities and continues to make decisions based on his own emotions despite current realities. In both instances, a decision will be made that is likely suboptimal and potentially calamitous. To avoid these issues, implement a structure that guides their work and ensures that they consider all of the essential factors.

Critical reasoning skills:

Recognize that a decision must be made: Clarify what you are choosing and why you are making the selection.

Determine the type of direction required for each circumstance: Is a fast decision more important than a precise one? These two are typically on opposite ends of the scale, and you must find the appropriate equilibrium. Try not to use an endless data social affair to defer difficult decisions, and don't make hasty decisions when something significant is at stake and you need more data to pursue the right choice.

Consider potential diverse outcomes for alternative choices: Having three fundamental outcomes is generally sufficient: the best-case scenario, the worst-case scenario, and the average outcome. Evaluate the risk-to-reward ratio objectively for each option. When you have everything you desire, choose immediately and commence execution.

Identifying the test: In this phase, the chief identifies a problem and determines its circumstances.

After acquiring additional information about the case, the administrator devises one or more prospective arrangements.

Considering choices: The administrator breaks down the advantages and disadvantages of each option and investigates optional arrangements as required.

Following a choice: After a thorough evaluation, the director reaches a final decision regarding what action to take.

Educating others regarding the selection, the director advises representatives regarding the selection and clarifies what the selection implies for the workplace.

Developing a Growth Mindset Among Your Team

Employees with a fixed mindset resist change and avoid challenges. They believe that their skills and abilities are unchangeable. You should avoid this and adopt a growth mindset instead. People with a growth mindset recognize their capacity for growth, learn from their mistakes, and comprehend what it takes to remain motivated. Above all else, a growth mindset enables us to recognize the potential in every individual, regardless of their origin.

Here are five methods for encouraging a growth mindset at work:

Connect performance assessment to learning, not output

Employees are more likely to adopt a growth mindset if their performance evaluations are based on learning rather than output. This is due to the fact that output is quantitative whereas performance evaluations are qualitative. In a performance evaluation, you can discuss the various skills an employee may wish to acquire through training, education, etc. On the contrary, output is dependent solely on increasing profits.

Focusing on quantitative profits does not motivate employees to do more or to work effectively or efficiently; it merely induces them to work harder. Improving qualitative skills and experience, on the other hand, increases long-term output and creates an employee who is more well-rounded, qualified, and motivated to continue to develop, to the benefit of the workplace.

Successes and Failures Are Opportunities for Learning

In numerous organizations, failures are frequently punished severely. Employees are hesitant to confess failure out of fear of termination or suspension. When employees believe that failures will be recorded on their permanent records, they are more likely to conceal them, causing problems for the organization. For instance, employees who fear retribution are unlikely to disclose the truth. They will develop a culture of reticence that will harm your organization.

As a leader, it is preferable to foster a workplace culture in which failures are viewed as opportunities to learn and perform better in the future. Thus, employees are provided with the mental and physical space to utilize their failures as learning opportunities. Likewise, successes should be celebrated not only as organizational successes but also as employee successes. Your employees will feel appreciated when you recognize their accomplishments, which will motivate them to learn and do more.

Give Employees the Opportunity to Speak Giving employees the opportunity to speak is crucial to creating an inclusive, secure environment for people from a variety of backgrounds. This open dialogue is also excellent for bolstering employee morale and fostering a positive work environment. People desire to be heard rather than commanded. Permit your employees to contribute to the company's ideas and resolutions.

Invest in Upskilling

It can be challenging for employees to find the time, money, and resources to invest in skill development. In addition, many organizations are hesitant to invest in upskilling for concern that employees will use their new skills to obtain higher-paying employment. Investing in upskilling, however, is an investment in your workforce. A worker with superior abilities will put those abilities to good use in your workplace. If you compensate your employees adequately for their time and effort in developing a new skill, you do not need to stress about them moving to a different workplace. In addition to upskilling your employees, you can retain them by providing leadership opportunities where they can put their new skills to use.

Support Individual Learning and Learning Across Domains

When someone begins a new position at a company, it can be difficult to identify opportunities for advancement. Cross-domain learning enables your employee to temporarily transfer to a different team and expand their expertise if they are interested in assisting with a variety of projects. When a team identifies what they are impassioned about, productivity is significantly enhanced. When employees have a better understanding of their colleagues' responsibilities, a greater appreciation and clearer vision of the company's accomplishments can result. Providing your employee with one-on-one learning opportunities with a respected peer or with you as a coach can also help them expand their future objectives within the organization as they discover new opportunities.

Chapter 7: A Discussion Of Leadership

This chapter discusses both the definition of a leader and the various authority options available to leaders. You will concur that leaders can be found in both formal and informal organizations. In this situation, determining how they gain influence over their subordinates is crucial.

We define a leader as someone who motivates a group of people to act in a particular manner in order to attain a particular objective. In this context, leadership is the process by which an individual enlists the support and assistance of others to accomplish a common objective or purpose. It involves establishing the framework for individuals to contribute to a particular objective. Obviously, there are varieties of leadership that fall into the categories of effective and ineffective.

The ability to influence vast numbers of people is only desirable if it is on the correct path, so effective leadership is our top priority. Effective leadership requires the capacity to integrate and optimize the internal and external resources available to attain social or organizational objectives.

There are numerous leadership theories addressing various aspects of leadership. It is essential to recognize that leadership does not necessarily imply formal authority. However, a person must possess specific abilities in order to influence their adherents or peers, or even to control resources. It is essential for a successful leader to utilize these capabilities to influence his subordinates or followers effectively. To enhance the effectiveness of their leadership, leaders would need to comprehend how power is utilized.

There are numerous types of capabilities, such as:

Coercion is the authority a person derives from their capacity to threaten punishment against their followers. The majority of the time, leaders in organizations have the authority to suspend their adherents, employees, or subordinates. This power guarantees excellent tracking, but it does not always come with affection or esteem. In most instances, subordinates follow a superior out of fear of retaliation, not out of their own volition, will, or impulse. Using this type of authority over subordinates is reviled by society. However, this does not diminish its value in ensuring that an organization's mission is fulfilled and that quality work is performed.

Frequent in organizational systems, this type of authority is unique to organizations. In this circumstance, a person's authority is constrained by their level of influence within the group, team, or organization. This highlights the significance of organizational hierarchy, as a person's authority increases with their position.

This type of power, which is most commonly found in formal institutions or organizations, is held by a leader who has the authority to award subordinates with rewards. Due to the enticement they are dangling in this circumstance, they will influence the decisions of their subordinates. These incentives, which frequently take the form of promotions or pay raises, are granted to subordinates who have demonstrated exceptional performance on the job. In situations where the reward system is for individuals, people may draw in different directions to outsmart one another, but this has the effect of uniting them around a common goal or purpose.

Despite the fact that the task would still be completed, it can occasionally lead to disagreements if the framework for rewards is deemed to be unjust. When favoritism is present, it may have the opposite effect of uniting the group and cause discord instead.

People with charismatic influence can be found in both formal and informal groups. In this situation, the leader's ability to appeal to the emotions of the followers assures their immediate devotion, love, and even fanaticism. The charisma of the leader can have a positive effect on the followers, especially during addresses. This has the potential to be one of the most beneficial abilities for completing a task because followers can relate to the leader for interpersonal impact. The capacity of a leader to communicate with the emotions of his or her followers confers immense influence on them.

This is a possibility in both official and informal groups. Due to their knowledge, talents, abilities, or experience, this individual appears to be potent in this situation. In order to remain pertinent, a leader must have a specific level of experience that others do not possess. This leader consistently makes substantial contributions to the business or organization for which he works.

The influence of information is not dissimilar to the power of experts. However, in this instance, the leader possesses information that would enhance the organization's operation or the achievement of social objectives. One thing you will observe is that this power is not contingent on hierarchy, as individuals at lower levels of the hierarchy may possess greater informational power. This does not diminish its potency. In fact, they recognize it as one of the most genuine forms of influence, whose viability derives from information.

This type of influence is derived from the connection between two individuals. People in this context use the terms assistant and associate. It is not always a reliable form of power, especially when it comes to persuading people to work toward a common objective.

Chapter 8: How to Develop Leadership Abilities and Become an Outstanding Leader

Even the most novice members of a team can learn to be effective leaders if they use their talents to motivate and assist their teams in moving forward and ultimately achieving their goals (individually, departmentally, and enterprise-wide). Moreover, leadership can be exercised in a variety of contexts outside the workplace, including religious communities, volunteer communities, and neighborhood communities, among others. Even if your sphere of influence is comparatively small, you can contribute significantly to the success of the organization.

Leadership is not exclusive to those at the summit of an organization's hierarchy, nor is it limited to those who possess what are commonly considered to be leadership qualities (such as an outgoing personality, for example). It's also essential to note that although we often refer to leadership as a singular skill, it's actually a collection of skills (most of which can be developed through experience and training) that are uniquely influenced by a person's personality and background. Consider your own experience: it's likely that the leaders you've interacted with throughout your life have exhibited a variety of leadership styles. However, the majority of them possessed a similar set of effective leadership traits from which they drew.

Fortunately, unlike some highly specialized or technical skills, leadership is a competency that is accessible to everyone, regardless of where they fall on an organizational chart; similarly, anyone can develop leadership skills, whether through formal training or through self-education and practice on the job.

For instance, if you are a relatively novice member of your organization, you may want to evaluate your performance on each of the aforementioned leadership qualities. Perhaps you'll recognize some of them as characteristics you already possess, and perhaps you'll identify others as areas for improvement. This could involve exercising active listening during meetings with coworkers, being proactive in bringing new ideas to your team, or requesting assistance from a peer or manager to improve one of your weaker areas.

If you want to be considered for a promotion or a job change into a higher-level position (or if you're already in a management role and want to hone your leadership skills to be as successful as possible), you might want to consider obtaining a more formal education or training in leadership. There are numerous programs available, ranging from short-term leadership seminars to full-degree programs, that can assist you in becoming a visionary, transformational leader and achieving greater career success. Clearly, the education you receive will be more in-depth the lengthier and more in-depth the program is.

Chapter 9: Achievement Of Objectives: The Power Of Motivation And Dedication

Motivation and commitment are essential elements that can aid in the accomplishment of an objective. According to research, those who are motivated and committed to their objectives are typically more successful than those who are not.

Individuals who were more motivated to accomplish their goals were more likely to exert the necessary effort and work harder to achieve those goals, according to one study. Moreover, those who were more committed to their objectives were more likely to persevere and continue to work towards their objectives despite obstacles or setbacks.

Individuals who were highly motivated and committed to their objectives were more likely to experience greater well-being and life satisfaction, according to another study. This may be due to the fact that the process of pursuing and achieving one's objectives can provide a sense of purpose and meaning, which can be essential to one's overall well-being.

Overall, the research indicates that being motivated and committed to working towards one's objectives is crucial to achieving success and living a fulfilling life.

Consider that your comments may be recorded, uploaded to YouTube, and circulated globally; therefore, say what you intend and mean what you say. There is no going back on it.

When a political strategy is misogynistic, it can be dangerous to question its foundation. When she was only eleven years old, Pakistani student Malala Yousafzai addressed the press club in Peshawar, asking, "How dare the Taliban remove my fundamental right to education?" Four years later, she was shot in the head while riding the school bus home. She adapted extraordinarily well and garnered worldwide acclaim as a result. Malala has effectively become a symbol and is worshipped as the youngest recipient of the Nobel Peace Prize.

Establish a Relationship with Your Audience

At the podium, women speakers have a few advantages over males. Some female characteristics, such as respect for others' perspectives and sociability, can be speaker qualities. The majority of research has found that women converse with one another to exchange information and form attachments. They remain receptive to what the audience has to say because of their beliefs. Generally, female speakers will provide information to assist audience members in achieving their objectives, rather than to establish dominance over the group or arrange status. In addition, if audience members become agitated, female speakers can quickly change direction because, on the platform as well as in everyday life, women are better at reading nonverbal cues than males.

Women identify with their counterparts through personal anecdotes, which can foster a sense of closeness. In addition, audiences enjoy hearing a speaker share a social illustration or insight gained from an extraordinary journey. A personal encounter can be instructive and politicizing for women. For instance, I heard a speaker who had been a parental figure begin an approach speech by answering her own question, "What have you learned about our medical care system from caring for a friend or family member with a chronic illness?" The audience was immediately drawn to her sincerity.

19. Versatility

Versatility enables leaders to adapt to a variety of circumstances.

Leaders must be sufficiently ferocious to fight, sufficiently sensitive to weep, sufficiently human to make mistakes, sufficiently humble to admit them, sufficiently resilient to endure stress, and sufficiently adaptable to return swiftly and continue to move.

Prior to having a sense of ownership with others, one must first have a firm grip on oneself. Adaptable leaders are perceptive and know how to handle themselves in any favorable or unfavorable circumstance. Versatile leaders are able to maintain their stamina under pressure and adapt to challenging situations. In addition, they overcome difficult obstacles without behaving horribly or injuring others. Tough leaders are high-performing leaders who overcome any obstacle resolutely.

20. Responsibility Exceptional leaders are by nature responsible Being a responsible leader is not a simple assignment. It implies that you can assume responsibility for your

responsibilities and obligations. It entails being accountable for the actions and decisions made by yourself and those you oversee. Leaders with integrity articulate their objectives and goals with clarity. They are focused on the future and acknowledge their mistakes. They request assistance when necessary and provide valid and valuable feedback.

Strong A-strong leader directing his or her colleague Leadership without assistance is comparable to endeavoring to construct bricks without sufficient straw. Genuine leaders construct their ideas and plans with the assistance of vital institutions, alliances, and large populations.

Constant leaders provide the desired direction. Consistent leaders instruct and guide you until you require almost no supervision in the future. They lack confidence in assigning tasks and expecting immediate results. They are always present and provide support through their knowledge and experiences. In order to maintain a high level of cooperation, strong leadership entails fostering a culture of trust amongst coworkers and encouraging open communication. In this manner, the fundamentals of consistent leadership are fostering cooperation, establishing connections, and accepting responsibility.

Well-informed A well-informed leader holding a telephone and a computer next to a table with a computer.

For sophisticated change, the world requires Technologically-Aware leaders. To support their organization, the current leader must have a sufficient understanding of innovation. The association's innovation decisions should be guided by a system and its manual experience should be digitized. Currently, the majority of organizations are highly developed, and this trend will continue to expand significantly over time. Therefore, it is evident that business executives must enhance their innovative abilities for maintainability and making better decisions.

A compassionate leader communicating with a colleague to perceive his perspective.

Empathy is a central leadership attribute that helps you support your team. Understanding the needs and thought processes of others is the essence of empathy. We live in a world with a consistent correspondence circle, and individuals collaborate with one another in a very straightforward manner. Nevertheless, individuals have less compassion for one another. Many communicate for the purpose of conveying their thoughts, as opposed to understanding those of others.

Leaders with empathy are perceptive and aware of others' feelings and thoughts. Being empathetic does not typically entail agreeing with others' viewpoints, but rather a willingness to appreciate and comprehend them.

24. Learning Agility

A dexterous leader perusing a stack of books while perched on a pile of books.

Leaders with dexterity respond most effectively to authoritative change and vulnerability. Today, we require leaders who are more adept at navigation and can act swiftly in times of crisis. We live in a fast-paced world where work patterns change in a matter of seconds. Consequently, there is little time for everyone to make decisive decisions. Similarly, systems and strategies that were effective in the past may be obsolete today. The Covid-19 emergency is one of the distinguishable variants. The emergency had altered the work environment, and executives needed to find new strategies to combat the tempest in the short term.

The ultimate consequence of work will always be uncertain and debatable. Future events will present fresh challenges. Associations will only flourish in the future under the management of leaders who can manage vulnerability.

25. Strengthening

A leader with exceptional leadership qualities who enables his group to cooperate.

Incredible leaders can motivate their teams to achieve the highest levels of productivity and authority.

Strengthening provides colleagues with equivalent dynamic opportunities and utilizes their judgment and expertise to nurture arrangements. This creates a sense of individual worth and a sense of obligation to the organization among representatives. Each person offers abilities and talents of genuine worth that frequently lead to the discovery of a stream. You likely have accomplished coworkers, but a lack of direction and inspiration prevents you from giving them your best.

It is therefore the responsibility of leaders to cultivate these skills through engagement. Great leaders are able to inspire positive traits in others. They recognize that the most effective method is to engage them. In this manner, leaders embrace persistently engaging individuals and strengthening the group as an everyday practice.

Chapter 10: Leadership Is Internal

Leaders are not innate. They are socialized. Previous research indicates that leadership has a remarkably small genetic component. (University of Illinois College of Agricultural, Consumer, and Environmental Sciences [ACES], 2014) Research indicates that leadership is a taught skill and that genetics only account for 30% of the picture. The research results are encouraging because they suggest that anyone can acquire the necessary leadership skills with the proper guidance.

In our fast-paced, digital-first world, leadership abilities are in high demand. These talents are applicable to any industry or position. Developing the appropriate leadership abilities can make the difference between career advancement and stagnation. (Indeed

Editorial Team, 2021a) Leadership abilities encompass a wide variety of skills, attributes, and personality traits. Good leaders will have a diverse skill set that will suit them well in a variety of positions. Effective leaders endeavor to develop the following essential abilities:

These competencies center on the ability to establish objectives while keeping the large picture in mind. Setting goals is done for the benefit of the company, project, or team as a whole, and can involve a series of smaller and larger goals as well as the actions required to achieve these objectives. Setting goals should make use of the available resources within your team and must be attainable.

Transmission and delegation: Effective communication skills not only improve our contemporaries' ability to comprehend us, but also aid leaders in determining the optimal mode of communication for particular messages. Some topics are best discussed face-to-face, while others can be readily addressed via email. An effective communicator is aware of which mode of communication will most effectively convey their message. Similarly crucial is the ability to delegate. No leader is expected to do everything alone; therefore, refining your delegation skills can free up valuable time in a hectic environment. Ensure that the instructions are clear and task-specific when delegating, and choose the team member or employee who is best qualified for the task.

Integrity and dependability: Dependability refers to the degree of confidence we have in someone to complete a task accurately and on time. This quality can be fostered by establishing a work ethic standard that emphasizes punctuality, courtesy, and leading by example for your team. Integrity is a necessary component of leadership by example. Leaders must accept responsibility for their actions and errors and promote an honest culture.

The ability to make educated decisions rapidly, even when under pressure, is a valuable trait. Effective leaders recognize that certain decisions cannot be postponed and that certain situations require immediate action. This does not imply that these leaders disregard the possible outcomes of their decisions. Instead, they strive to minimize potentially negative outcomes by making quality decisions quickly based on their industry knowledge and experience. This ability develops naturally as you acquire experience in your chosen industry.

Motivation and conflict resolution: The ability to motivate others is essential, particularly when team members must rally to complete tasks and achieve objectives. Self-motivation holds equal importance. You cannot expect your team to be motivated and diligent if the leader is a procrastination maestro! The key to maintaining others' motivation is conflict management. This skill enables leaders to be effective mediators when the situation calls for it; the need for conflict management can arise surprisingly frequently, particularly when people have differing perspectives on a situation or topic. Achieving a reasonable compromise for all parties requires this skill.

Identifying the assets and weaknesses of our teams is essential to achieving our goals and objectives. Teamwork is required to achieve these objectives. Team building is utilized by leaders to foster collaboration within their organizations. These training and team-building exercises help our coworkers get to know one another better, fostering a culture of respect.

Chapter 11: On The Shoulders Of Titans

After spending a year with the Carters in Big River, I returned to British Columbia to spend a few weeks with my grandmother and companions before returning to Saskatchewan. This time it was to the southern portion of the province and a new way of life: dormitory life at a Bible school. I attended for only one year, but during that time I received solid biblical instruction from devoted teachers, helped pioneer a coffeehouse ministry to reach community teenagers with the gospel, and listened to visiting speakers who were making a difference on a global scale.

Our dean of women was a towering missionary with gray hair who became a widow on the mission field. She returned home with her two children and quickly earned a reputation for being strict and uncompromising among the school's students and faculty. It didn't take long for me to realize that she saw through my subtle rebellion whenever I pressed the rule book's boundaries or initiated dorm shenanigans. Her example taught me that a calm response is frequently more effective than a lengthy lecture and forbidding expression, although both have their place. She also taught me that a person's inner state influences her behavior, even when she is acting foolishly.

Her subtle smile in response to our dorm pranks revealed to me that fun is enjoyable, but a person must be accountable for the outcome of the fun. She left an indelible mark on me and became another pair of shoulders in a long line of titans God used to shape me into the individual he knew was there but I had not yet seen.

At the conclusion of the academic year, I returned home to spend the summer with my grandmother and to assist Len Roberts, the first youth pastor at my home church, as his volunteer assistant. This experience initiated an enduring friendship with Len and Jean, as well as years of ministry collaboration. While renovating the ancient section of the church and transforming it into a coffeehouse and youth center, we also generated ideas. Len taught me how to plan strategically. To think creatively and organize teams so that they are focused on a vision. To view ministry and daily life as a single entity, rather than as two distinct aspects of existence.

In the autumn, when the Missing Link Coffeehouse opened, I knew I would not return to Bible school. Instead, I obtained a paid position and continued to volunteer at the church, where we saw more than three hundred teenagers enter the coffeehouse on weekends. I continued to assist Len and eventually became the percussionist for the house band, which began performing at other churches and outdoor youth events. It was a time of learning and service, of being at the forefront and making a difference. I also enjoyed it.

During this period, a friendship developed with a handsome sailor. When I was sixteen, we first met, but we went our separate ways before reuniting a year later. Jim's demeanor contradicted people's preconceived notions of someone who donned a leather jacket and rode a motorcycle. His hair was black and his eyes were dark, deeply set, and kind. I was captivated by his tall, erect stature and delicate, yet edgy allure. He volunteered with us at the coffeehouse after leaving the military, apprenticing as a bricklayer, and desiring to serve God. We were wedded in 1971, and a new adventure began. I was twenty-one while he was twenty-four.

A month after our wedding, Jim told me he had stayed up all night because he believed God wanted him to attend college. Over the next two years, we witnessed God's provision through miracle after miracle. We continued to volunteer at the coffeehouse while I worked on campus, he attended courses and performed odd jobs, and we continued to volunteer at the coffeehouse.

As Jim was about to begin his third year, Len Roberts approached us with an offer that would eternally alter the course of our lives. "I've resigned from the church, and I'd like you to consider taking a year off from school to help launch a ministry that reaches out to disadvantaged adolescents and young offenders. What are your thoughts?

After discussion and prayer, we decided to take action. God continued to hone my skills, refine my walk with him, and extend my faith as I participated in the One Way Adventure Foundation's new boot camp. However, it would not be without obstacles.

Chapter 12: How Do You Attract Precisely What You Desire?

Need to attract precisely what you require? Indeed, everything in the universe consists of energy, including you. In addition, the first step you should take to attract the items you need is to shift or alter your energy.

Individuals comprehend your motivation. If it is positive, you will only attract positive circumstances and people into your life. Nonetheless, if it is negative energy, you will consistently attract only negative circumstances and gloomy people into your existence.

If you feel that you are receiving things that you could do without or that you are not receiving things that you genuinely need in your daily life, then there is a high probability that you are shipping off-base energy.

How could you reverse the situation?

If you want to transform your cynicism into an abundance of vitality in your daily life, you must alter the way you perceive the world. Start discarding your negative convictions and negative thoughts. This will alter your inner essence. This will allow you to attract the items you require most.

This fundamental entails that you must focus on the positive circumstances, comprehend and accept that everything will turn out well, search for answers to your concerns and stop whining, transform yourself into a seriously determining individual, embrace the truth and the essence of progress, and search for the open doors instead of focusing on your worries. Stop accepting that the worst possible outcomes will occur.

The Challenges of Connecting in Chapter 2

As a leader, you must always remember that everyone needs

encouragement. And everyone who receives it—whether young or old, successful or unsuccessful, unknown or well-known—is affected by it. —John C. Maxwell

No one ever claimed that leadership was simple. In fact, if you're doing leadership correctly, it should be the most difficult and rewarding position in the organization. No one who desires an easy position or a comfortable promotion should pursue leadership. Typically, it entails more hours, more complex problems, and greater responsibility for these issues. As expected, becoming an effective leader requires years of education and training. No one immediately perfects their leadership abilities, so be patient with yourself!

Nevertheless, as we discussed in the introduction, stereotypes frequently prevent certain individuals from gaining experience or acquiring new skills. Professional advancement opportunities for women are frequently obstructed in male-dominated workplaces, specifically in leadership positions. This gatekeeping can take formal forms, such as excluding women from promotions and professional conferences. It can be informal, as in the case of male employees who have informal networks based on male bonding, or the succession-based mentorship dynamic in which bosses favor male subordinates as protégés. Some women obstruct the advancement of other women out of envy, fear of losing their hard-won position, or unwillingness to deal with the "drama," i.e. the emotions women share.

Women can also impede their own professional advancement due to impostor syndrome, fear of criticism, or even failure phobia. These anxieties frequently prevent us from seeking promotions or launching businesses. In either case, these negative beliefs are founded on the premise that women cannot be leaders.

Limiting women's opportunities creates a viscous cycle, as it prevents women from acquiring the necessary skills to even request promotions. By denying to teach women adequate leadership skills, workplaces perpetuate the notion that women are less qualified for leadership positions than men, despite the fact that these men have received significantly more training and mentoring opportunities. This occurrence has occurred previously. Prior to the 20th century, women were not permitted to attend universities where they could study professions such as medicine and engineering, limiting their earning potential. Throughout history, the gatekeeping of education has been used as a tool to keep women in low-status positions, working more hours for less pay with no upward mobility opportunities.

But where did this preconception regarding female leaders originate? It is not supported by any credible research. Numerous studies indicate that, when given the chance, women thrive in leadership positions much more than their male counterparts. Prime Minister of New Zealand Jacinda Ardern exemplifies that when women lead, they do so in their own manner and with their own set of skills. The connected leadership skills covered in Chapter 1 are examples of uniquely female leadership styles that can entirely invert traditional leadership practices.

There is nothing biological that prevents women from leadership, and throughout history, women have led in a variety of contexts. There are evident examples, such as female presidents and prime ministers and empire-leading queens. However, even outside the realm of politics, female leadership has been a pillar of society. In numerous cultures, the marketplace is viewed as a female domain and serves as the economic hub of numerous societies. In the seventh century, Shifa Abdulla, a companion of the Prophet Muhammad, was in command of the entire marketplace in Madinah, the capital of the Islamic Empire. Women in the Igbo culture of Nigeria have historically managed the vast markets that comprise West African commerce. This does not even include teaching or family life, which have historically been arenas in which women have held strong leadership positions, such as task delegation and conflict resolution. Women have performed significant leadership roles throughout history, even when they have not been elected or crowned rulers.

As we can see, there has not always been a prejudice against women leaders, at least not everywhere. The difficulties women confront in the workplace today are a result of our current culture and its gender stereotypes. Narratives such as female fragility, lack of conflict resolution skills, inability to be stern or firm, and difficulty gaining the respect of male subordinates all impede women's advancement in the workforce today. Leadership can be an extremely challenging task, but it is achievable. Although this article focuses on the workplace, you can also be an inspiring leader in your social circles, at home, and in any other context in which you inspire others and assume responsibility. This chapter will examine how women can overcome gender stereotypes and biases to become the most effective leaders possible.

Chapter 13: The Importance Of Leadership Principles

Leadership principles are significant because they establish the organization's tone and culture. If the organization is to be run by the seat of its trousers, these principles will be rendered useless because they will be disregarded. Leaders must inspire confidence in their followers. Leadership principles define the qualities of effective leaders. Potential leaders who do not exhibit these characteristics can be swiftly identified as those who require additional training and development. Alternatively, they may not be suitable for leadership at all.

A leadership principle is a fundamental rule, established behavior, or policy that should be adhered to. It is meant to be an integral component of something. Consequently, in a business organization, these principles represent how the business should operate and how individuals should lead and represent the organization. The application of leadership principles ensures that both the leadership style of an organization and the leaders themselves are predicated on sound concepts and techniques. They will naturally steer leaders away from undesirable characteristics and conduct.

If sound leadership principles have been established, the organization can assess and measure performance more precisely. No one can be held responsible for something that has not been communicated explicitly. Thus, leadership principles are frequently included in an organization's written operational procedures.

Why do reputable organizations place so much emphasis on leadership standards? Because they provide controls and a framework for conducting business that, according to the organization, will provide the greatest opportunity for business success. If leadership principles did not have value, they would not exist. However, successful companies have demonstrated that establishing these principles is advantageous and will provide an organization with the greatest opportunity for success.

These principles intrinsically characterize the organization's core values. They indicate the organization's priorities and how it intends to operate. The objective is to provide the best possible products and services to consumers by providing the best possible environment for leaders and employees. Products and services will tend to be overcharged if quality is not a significant factor. If customer service is not prioritized, customers will experience frustration when interacting with a business.

Because leadership is the responsibility of all employees and adherents, the principles of leadership apply to everyone in the organization. Everyone is a leader in some capacity, so this is true. Even the president and CEO are not exempt from these principles. Leaders are role models. These principles permeate the entire organization, from the executive suite to the mail room.

These principles foster an environment that enables the organization to compete effectively in the market. However, the principles also shape and strengthen the personalities and abilities of individuals. Good products that others desire to acquire are the result of good individuals performing good work.

Success may be defined differently by various individuals, especially those at various organizational levels. As one ascends the management hierarchy within an organization, the objectives become more expansive. At the top, there is a heightened focus on the organization's expected financial performance over the next five to ten years. Numerous CEOs are wholly preoccupied with the future and only occasionally consider the current year.

We have chosen to discuss the following principles because we consider them to be the most crucial. These are listed in no particular order, with the exception of the first principle, which we perceive to be the most crucial to leadership success overall.

Chapter 14: What Is Business Culture?

Indeed defines company culture as a set of behavioral or procedural norms observed within the organization (Indeed, n.d.). These norms establish expectations or guidelines for how employees (at all hierarchical levels) interact with one another, perform their jobs, and advance within the organization. From a managerial standpoint, company culture influences the leadership style, company policies, employee expectations, disciplinary action, and various rewards or benefits designed to make employees feel valued and appreciated.

Whether or not you are aware of it, your organization has already established a culture. You may not have intentionally created the culture, but by making certain business decisions and responding to challenges in a particular manner, you were creating one. Many executives believe, incorrectly, that company culture only affects how employees are treated. Every facet of a business is influenced by company culture, including the following five factors:

1. Executive

Your company's culture determines the type of relationships you cultivate with employees, your decision-making process, and the methods you use to recognize employee performance. If you have a healthy company culture, you will observe that employees are at ease interacting with managers, have the freedom to express their opinions, and have a favorable perception of the company.

Workplace Procedures

The company culture enforces daily work processes, systems, policies, recruitment, and training. Depending on the organization's ethics, values, and objectives, certain rules and procedures will be emphasized more or less. For instance, if achieving a healthy work-life balance is a priority for your organization, you might construct employee-friendly rules regarding work schedules.

3. Persons

Developing a distinct company culture can be extremely advantageous during the recruitment and induction processes. For instance, based on your company's culture, you can search for candidates with specific soft and hard skills, as well as someone whose values and personality align with your organization's goals.

Vision, mission, and values of the company

A company's culture is closely linked to its vision, mission, and core values. In most circumstances, the company's vision and mission statement inspire the optimal organizational culture. If diversity is one of the most important company objectives, for instance, management will ensure that diversity is incorporated into company policy, ethics, and work life.

5. Communication

The company's culture influences the manner in which employees communicate with one another at work. Some organizations, for instance, place a premium on work teams; consequently, employee collaboration is crucial to attaining the team's objectives. Other companies may place a premium on openness and responsibility, and as a result, hold regular catch-up sessions with management to inform employees of the most recent updates or forthcoming organizational developments.

Consider the type of company ethos that your organization currently possesses. Would you say that this culture aligns with your mission, vision, and core values? Does it make employees feel secure and optimistic about their potential for advancement within the organization? If not, now is the time to consider methods to modify your company's culture and create a work environment that reduces employee turnover and attracts qualified applicants!

Chapter 15: Other Assessment Systems

During the middle of the 1990s, Myers-Briggs gained popularity. So that we could better comprehend each other, the president of Ameritech Cellular brought in a consultant to test mid- and upper-level managers. I was eager to discover more about myself, my colleagues, and my teams. My results confirmed what I already knew, namely that my personality type is an introvert with a strategic, logical way of thinking who prefers to concentrate on abstract information over concrete details. This has left me with many concerns.

Although the information about my coworkers was beneficial, it did not alter my interactions with them. I was able to recognize our distinctions, but I did not receive instructions on how to interact with them more effectively. And I became disillusioned when I observed individuals manipulating the test.

It was common knowledge within the company that the president favored outgoing and forceful individuals. Despite admitting to being an introvert, my supervisor answered the Myers-Briggs questions as if she were an extrovert when she took the test. The majority of these assessments, including DISC, rely on individuals responding a series of questions. Even when employees respond to the best of their abilities, their responses are frequently conditioned rather than genuine.

We all acquire beliefs, particularly as young children, from our families, instructors, and peers. Until these beliefs are observed and questioned, we are unaware that they are not ours. The lens through which we view the world is colored by these beliefs, which are similar to programs operating in our subconscious. Our responses to assessment queries are filtered through these beliefs.

I appreciate that companies recognize that individuals operate in a variety of ways and strive to learn more about their workers. Those were some of the finest tools available at the time, but I would have preferred a tool that was free of bias and didn't require a list of questions to be answered. Astrology can be helpful, but it appeared so convoluted that I had no desire to study it.

Chapter 16: Goal Setting

Everyone has unique objectives. However, establishing them is an art form. It is a delicate balance and an intriguing procedure. We all have goals we wish to accomplish. However, without setting objectives, these aspirations will remain aspirations. Not only must the objectives you set for yourself support the company's mission on the work front, but they must also reflect your own personal aspirations. If this condition is not met, the act of setting them becomes a matter of marking boxes.

A basic yet effective technique is to use the SMART technique. This involves establishing objectives that are SMART (Small, Measurable, Achievable, Relevant, and Time-Bound). If an objective does not satisfy all of these conditions, achieving it becomes more difficult. Regardless of how large or difficult a goal is, it can be broken down into simpler objectives. Similarly, if you are unable to measure your progress, it is nearly impossible to determine how far you have come or how much further you must travel to reach your goals. When an objective is quantifiable, it is possible to take the necessary steps to effect change. Additionally, it must be attainable. There is no purpose in pursuing unattainable goals. In actuality, it is a formula for failure. The objective must be relevant or valuable to you. If this element is lacking, the necessary motivation to continue diminishes, especially when obstacles arise. This decreases the likelihood of success. Lastly, the objective must be time-sensitive. Without a deadline or a set amount of time to complete a task, procrastination and other distractions take precedence. Before implementing any of the suggestions in this chapter, you must first establish SMART objectives.

Obtain Clarity

Prior to establishing your intended goals, you must have a clear understanding of your managerial function, responsibilities, and purpose. Unless you are aware of all of the above, the objective will be irrelevant. Prior to endeavoring to take an organization to the next level, it is logical to have a clear understanding of your mission's purpose - something that many fail to do despite having the best of intentions. Additionally, you must ensure that your objectives do not interfere with your work or your managerial duties. Instead, they must be in complete harmony with these considerations. Therefore, you need clarity before you can begin. Without this, it will be difficult to achieve any objective you set. Once you have a clear understanding of the specific and quantifiable things you can improve or learn, your likelihood of success will increase automatically.

Engage Others

Two minds are superior to one when it comes to solving problems. When attempting to establish goals or recognizing that you are struggling to do so, conversing with others is always beneficial. It need not be members of your team. You can instead communicate with your superiors or colleagues. Consult with other administrators at the same level as you. Conversation with them will provide you with a variety of perspectives on potential areas of focus. The input of others can define your objectives. As a result of your current course of thought, you may not even be aware of the opportunities you have overlooked or considered. Ultimately, seeking assistance or support from individuals outside your immediate professional circle can introduce you to a world of knowledge and expertise, thereby enhancing your ability to plan clear and attainable long-term objectives.

Elements You Can Control

In order to set and achieve objectives, you will need a plan of action. This plan must take into account both the elements that you can control and those that you cannot. Despite the difficulty, this is required to increase your odds of success. You need not be overly concerned about factors or elements that you cannot control. You must instead plan and prepare for them. When you are prepared, even if it is only mental preparedness, your ability to overcome the obstacle, challenge, or problem you encounter in the future increases; this ensures that you stay on course and do not become sidetracked. It also prevents you from losing motivation while pursuing the stated objective.

Chapter 17: You Must Understand That Your Goal Is Greater Than Your Challenges

You must always keep in mind that your purpose transcends your struggles. Everything necessary for success, success, and productivity in the sphere of addiction has already been implanted within you. So if you find yourself in a place where you feel a little discouraged and the people you are helping in your recovery facilities and your substance abuse facilities in any facility where you are working with different individuals, if you find that you are having difficulties and you are not seeing the fruit that you believe you are pouring into your clients and your recovery and your participants, do not give up.

If you become disheartened, avoid settling there. Remember that you already possess everything you need to be successful and productive in this discipline. It is known as an inside operation. I like to let people know that if you want to engage the public in what you're doing when you're attempting to build a community, you're going to face some form of resistance and struggle. I'm referring to outside of the organization for which you work.

When you attempt to engage them in what you are doing, you will encounter resistance. But don't despair. When attempting to manage or interact with individuals and provide them with professional services, always keep in mind that your purpose is more important than your struggles. There will be some individuals who will not accept your professional services regardless of how you present them with the opportunity. But I need you to realize that regardless of whether they receive it or not, regardless of the difficulties you face or not, regardless of whether you are dealing with recovery and they are not receiving the services correctly, regardless of how you are presenting it to them, you must not become disheartened.

If you become disheartened, do not settle there. Remember that your purpose transcends your struggles. I do not know who will undergo this training or who will read Season two, which corresponds to team number two. However, I need you to realize that your purpose is greater than your difficulties.

I must keep hammering that into your head because I need you to understand that I have encountered circumstances with my clients in which it appeared I was having a difficult time getting them to see what I needed them to see in order to be successful in their recovery. Then I realized that I was not to blame for the strife. The conflict is not my concern.

Frequently, I had to remind myself that the purpose of my efforts to assist them is greater than any difficulties I, the recovery, the participant, or the client may be experiencing. I am attempting to convince you of this as well. Always remember that your reason for being in that field is greater than any difficulty you may face in that field, and that there is something greater in every apple.

Everything necessary for success, success, and productivity in the field of addiction is already present within you. If you comprehend what I mean, the reason you are in that particular field is because it is the field that allows your heart to beat. So I will simply offer you encouragement.

And key number 2.5 is to concentrate on your reason for being in that profession. When attempting to engage the public in the substance abuse disorder treatment services you offer, you will encounter challenges. When attempting to provide the finest professional services possible to individuals, you will encounter resistance and struggle.

Some of them will reject your services regardless of how you present them or how professional they are.

These are known as difficulties. However, I need you to focus on the second essential, which is to recognize that your purpose is greater than your struggle. Listen to me. Each of us has been endowed with a unique spiritual aptitude.

The third bullet point. Each of us has been endowed with a unique spiritual aptitude. This simply means that it informs us that we have a particular talent, and that if we use it correctly, we will be able to observe the fruit of our investment in the lives of others. Each of us has a unique ability, and we do not need to be alike.

No matter who we are, we must utilize the skills and abilities that make us unique in order to complete the task. If you are participating in this peer recovery support and leadership training, you are doing so because you know you have something within you that you wish to pursue.

No one else possesses the same talent as you, which you use to assist another person, but you must maximize that talent. Each of us has been endowed with a unique spiritual gift. Now, let's proceed to the fourth bullet point to maximize your purpose. I am concentrating on purpose.

The second principle is that your purpose is greater than your struggle. The projectile force number. To maximize your goal, you must ask yourself the following three questions. You view it on the screen in order to maximize your intent. These are the required topics. The initial question is, "What is my current situation?" What's my desired destination, and third, what are the steps in between for you to maximize the purpose that you have in your life, if you're in the field of addiction and if you're taking this leadership training, then I know you're in the field of addiction, social service, mental health, or a similar field dealing with a criminal lifestyle.

You may be in the field of reentry, rehabilitation, or something else to maximize the purpose. Remember that I stated we all received the gift. This specific gift is our objective. To maximize this objective, we must ask ourselves the following three questions. What exactly are they?

Good topic. And I'm pleased you asked. The initial question is, "What is my current situation?"

Where do we stand?

What is my intended location?

Where are you attempting to acquire them?

And the third is, what are my intermediate steps?

If you use this specific teaching that I'm discussing right now, I used it with one of my recoveries in an effort to help them maximize their life's purpose. So I inquired as to their current circumstances.

He stated, "I am currently living in a sober living facility." I recently returned from rehabilitation. I am in a therapeutic living facility. I asked, "What is your desired location?" He stated, My desired destination is to obtain an apartment and a job. And I asked, what are the intermediate steps?

He says I must submit applications after obtaining employment. I am required to save money, and I save enough. I must locate an apartment. I said You got it, buddy guy. The same principle can be applied to our existence. To maximize your goal, you must ask yourself the following three questions.

What is my current circumstance?

What is my intended destination and how will I get there?

This strategy is effective not only for our recoveries, our clients, and our participants, but also for us, the professionals. It also functions well when we are attempting to engage the public in our activities. We endeavor to improve our professional services.

This strategy will work regardless of how it is implemented. In order to maximize the effectiveness of this strategy, you must ask these three questions. What is my current circumstance? What is my desired destination, and what are the actions between the fifth and sixth bullets? It states that when pursuing your purpose, you must grow in these areas.

This is something you can use with your recovery clients or participants, regardless of the terminology employed at your facility: discipline, structure, integrity, character, and limits. If you develop in these areas as a professional, you will be better equipped to assist your clients. However, we are often so focused on assisting our clients that we neglect our own well-being.

This training, peer recovery support, and leadership training are intended to assist individuals in my field with the development of professional services, public engagement, and self-care. When you are pursuing your purpose, you are in that field for a specific reason.

Whatever profession you are in, you are there for a specific reason, which you are aware of. But you must develop discipline, structure, integrity, character, and boundaries in these areas. These are merely a few of the regions where development is desirable, and if you are already developed in some of these regions, that's fantastic.

However, I observed that I was frequently underdeveloped in some of these areas, and I was attempting to recover. And I realized that the reason I was unable to assist him in that area was because I lacked the necessary discipline at the time. When I was not focused on integrity and character, I did not have a structured existence.

I violated boundaries as well. And I am aware that sometimes this is the ethical thing to do, and we consider it in this manner. However, I constructed this in an attempt to assist individuals in entering the next stage of their existence. Addiction professional team number two, you must recognize that your purpose is greater than your struggles, regardless of the struggles you may be experiencing at your agency, in your personal life, with your participants or clients, or during recovery.

Always keep in mind that your purpose transcends your struggles. This simply denotes that the reason you are in that profession is greater than anything you may face in the future. Thank you very much. I am known as Sobia. I will see you in session three.

Chapter 18: What We Wish You to Learn From This Book

This book will help you define your values and character, as well as demonstrate how to transform those qualities into leadership success. Your character becomes your compass as you navigate the twists and turns of life and leadership. Nobody's path to leadership will be identical. We can all become more effective leaders, however, if we use our character as a foundation, evaluate our skills and abilities, and strive for continuous growth.

Both of us participated in the exercises outlined in this book and used (and continue to use) them to enhance our understanding and practice of leadership. Our conversations have assisted us in defining and refining our own personalities, thereby assisting us in becoming better leaders. We know from our own experience that if you take the time to reflect on and employ the exercises and underlying principles we've provided, you will achieve the same results.

Throughout the research and composition of this book, we kept returning to the same fundamental idea: Personality is significantly less important than principled character when it comes to leadership. It is not how you behave, but who you are that matters. By applying these principles and working diligently to improve, your leadership skills will develop and flourish. Similar to how exercising our bodies produces muscle, exercising our character develops our leadership abilities. Leadership requires discipline and effort; we must consciously choose to become better leaders.

We want to assist you in pausing to consider who you are, who you aspire to be, and how you should shape the foundation of your leadership. Leadership resembles an unfinished structure. No defined position or salary indicates that a leader is "done" If we achieve a top position, we must continue to maintain our leadership skills, just as a home requires constant upkeep. Strong leadership is more about continuously refining and perfecting one's abilities while retaining one's moral integrity. The purpose of this book is to provide the blueprint for your leadership foundation. From this foundation, an enduring structure of effective leadership will emerge.

FIRST CHAPTER THE DYNAMICS OF ORGANIZED POLITICS

A political-free organization is impossible to achieve. The human desire for dominance and control is inherent...

— Dr. Med Jones

Anthony stood in front of the restroom mirror, adjusting his tie for the hundredth time. Along with four of his platoon members, he resumed his new position as an Internal Sales Representative in the organization where he served as a member of the National Youth Service Corps over a year ago. His brilliance, commitment, and capacity for on-the-job learning distinguished him and prompted management to retain him after his year of service.

On his first day of work, he was inundated with congratulations.

"Congratulations, Anthony," said the speaker. His colleague Beatrice greeted him with a smile as he entered the office.

'Thank you'. He smiled in return.

After lunch on that day, Anthony received a Slack message from his unit leader, Mr. John, and met with him. There were already three other members of the Sales department present. A seat was offered to him.

"How was your first day on the job?"

'Fine, master. This experience has been incredible. He was smiling widely.

It ought to be. Regardless, you are not a stranger here. Mr. John made a gesture to steady himself on his seat. 'It is the third quarter of the year, and as you already know, the department has developed a sales and marketing strategy for the company in preparation for the following year. Therefore, I'm bringing you into the team to work alongside the individuals you see here and myself'.

'Thank you, gentleman. I am so appreciative of this opportunity. Anthony attempted to contain his enthusiasm in his voice.

"You're very welcome. You deserve this, and you have my unwavering support.

"That is extremely kind of you, sir. Thank you'.

Mr. John replied, "Thank you." It is now time for the execution. We are pressed for time. I would like everyone to draft a proposal to present to the board the following week. He thereby dismissed everyone.

Excited and restless, Anthony was unable to sleep that night. It was one thing to be retained after service, but quite another to promptly become a member of the team and draw the company's sales pitch. Another thought kept him awake as he tossed in his bed like a kite lost in the sky: he had to come up with a proposal of his own.

In the days that followed, Anthony devised a marketing strategy that would guarantee an increase in company sales the following year.

* * * * *

Anthony was unsure of Mr. John's response to the email he sent, but he was confident that his work was superb. Therefore, he continued to check his official mail for Mr. John's response, which ultimately arrived at the end of the workday.

'Received. I will review it and provide feedback.

Anthony exhaled with relief. If his proposition was selected as the ideal marketing strategy for the company, it would enhance his reputation. In a company that only rewarded intelligence, perseverance, and diligence, he knew he had to be intelligent and eager to seize every opportunity. Positioning himself and maximizing every opportunity, taking on duties that other corps members would not, and staying late after work earned him a permanent position after his service.

Anthony was unaware that company employees compete and manipulate their way to the summit. The competition to rise and earn promotions and favor was genuine, as was the struggle to do so. People were required to be as shrewd as a serpent, to place eyes on their backs and ears on the walls. Before granting trust, loyalty was assessed, and vice versa. canines ate canines!

Mr. John did not return Anthony's call the following day, nor in the days that followed. However, the day before the marketing plan presentation, he received an email that stated, "I read your pitch." It sounds great.

This is incredible! Please prepare your transparencies, as this will be presented by you.

I will cheer for you!

After perusing the mail, Anthony was overjoyed. It meant a great deal to him. On a positive note, he began his career.

As Mr. John concluded his presentation on presentation day, the boardroom erupted in applause, but Anthony's face was red with wrath. He made a fist to stop his hands from trembling uncontrollably. It resembled a nightmare. He scowled at Mr. John, who was receiving handshakes while grinning.

He felt betrayed by Mr. John, who had endorsed his work and asked him to make the introductory presentation while he rounded up as the unit chief. After the board applauded Anthony's presentation, Mr. John countered each of Anthony's points by explaining why implementing any of them would result in failure.

Anthony was most offended by Mr. John's highlighted remark, "While Mr. Anthony had good intentions, his proposal would negatively impact our sales in this competitive market."

Anthony had surveyed all of the boardroom's faces, and their affirmative nods had wounded him.

However, Mr. John supported this proposal. Or did he use him to boost his credibility with the board?' he wondered.

Therefore, whether you consume, drink, or do anything else, do everything for the glory of God - 1 Corinthians 10:31. Work is a necessary aspect of life, and it should be performed with a positive attitude. Be deliberate about how you handle each duty and how you interact with each coworker today. Because this is how one glorifies God.

www.ingramcontent.com/pod-product-compliance
Lightning Source LLC
Chambersburg PA
CBHW050251120526
44590CB00016B/2307